# LBJ:  the Can-Do President

by

Louann Atkins Temple

First published by Dog Ear Publishing
4010 W. 86th Street, Ste H
Indianapolis, IN 46268
www.dogearpublishing.net

ISBN: 978-1-4575-1632-0
Library of Congress Control Number: 2012921901

This book is printed on acid-free paper.

Printed in the United States of America

# Table of Contents

to
Annie, Andy, Taylor, John and Will –
I wrote this for you

# *Acknowledgements*

Thank you, Lynda Robb, Luci Johnson, Harry Middleton, Betty Sue Flowers, Will Davis, Rich Kriese, Mary Whitaker, Anne Bustard and Kathleen Niendorff. You read this book and offered helpful suggestions with generosity of spirit, respect for American history, devotion to the teaching of young people and just plain kindness.

Thank you, Mark Updegrove – you are the sine qua non of this book – and thank you to your knowledgeable staff, especially Parker Duffie and Balmore Lazo.

And, of course, thank you Larry, the most trustworthy advisor a wife could have.

He was many faceted, marvelous, contradictory, with a great natural intelligence, a showman, a man of unlimited hopes and beliefs in this country.

——Lady Bird Johnson

# *Introduction*

When Lyndon Johnson said, "He's a can-do man," or, "She's a can-do woman," he was offering his highest praise. He meant that he admired that person for setting out to do a job and doing it well. This whirlwind of a President worked harder than most people and achieved stunning success in much of what he tried. He matched his can-do spirit with compassion for those people of his country who were discriminated against because of the color of their skin, or who lacked such basics as food, housing, education, jobs, or safe neighborhoods.

A can-do spirit, however, was not enough to allow him to accomplish all he wanted to as President because he governed during a time of change and conflict in America and of war in Vietnam. Minorities were voicing their dissatisfaction with a democratic country in which they, as citizens, were not treated as fairly as whites. They wanted to be able to attend the same schools, to work at the same jobs, and not to be asked to sit at the backs of buses or drink from different water fountains or stay in different hotels. Meanwhile, many white Americans, who believed that the races should have the same opportunities, also thought that they should live as separate groups within the country as they always had. They called this "separate but equal." Minorities believed that "equal" meant "together," not "separate."

At the same time, young people were experimenting with new ways to dress and look and behave. Rather than obeying adults unquestioningly, they were saying, "We don't like your fighting a war," and, "We don't like your telling women they can't have the same jobs as men," and, "We don't like your excluding other races from your neighborhood."

Often, the parents of these youth could not understand their children's protests. They believed in obeying, not challenging authority, as they had been taught to do when they were children. They were shocked when their sons moved to another country rather than fight a war they did not believe in. They felt uncomfortable with women running large businesses or being engineers. They were alarmed when their children marched alongside blacks to protest segregation. These were not the traditional ways they had always known. These were ways of acting they had never seen before.

All America joined in a loud conversation as the generations argued back and forth about making new rules for their lives.

The President wanted to encourage good change, but he also wanted to keep the country safe and orderly. Sometimes people quit talking and carrying signs of protest and started rioting-- throwing things and hurting each other. Sometimes those who objected to the protests also let their anger get out of control. Sometimes, as a result, the President had to bring in soldiers to maintain order. His job was to keep his country peaceful while allowing its citizens to talk about their problems in a way that was good for the country and not destructive.

Being a can-do person is not only about succeeding. It is also about continuing to try no matter how tough the odds. This is the story of a man who, in angry, troubled times, never quit struggling to solve his country's problems and never gave up his dream of making it a better place for all its citizens. That's a can-do man.

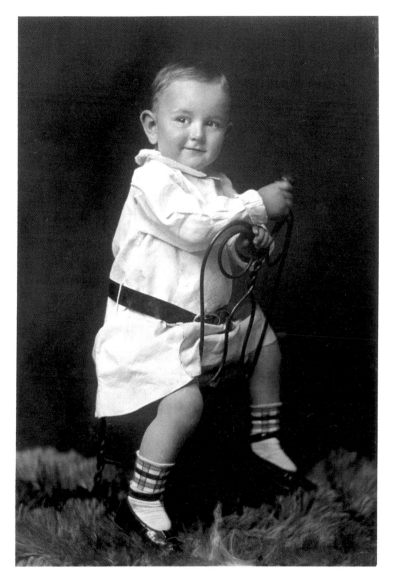

1910, Lyndon is 18 months old

# CHAPTER I

## *The Young Lyndon Johnson*

LYNDON BAINES JOHNSON, from Texas, became the 36th President of the United States in 1963. Americans called him "LBJ." This Texas-cowboy-looking man stood 6 feet 3 inches tall and wore a Stetson hat. He combed his hair straight back from his face, which was lined and sunbrowned from growing up on a farm. When he talked to people, he stood close to them and looked deep into their eyes, often trying with words and his oversize presence to convince them to join him in action. He paid close and serious attention to all that he did, and he had the energy and curiosity to do much. When he was not working, he did not like to be alone; he wanted his family and friends around him all the time for fast-moving conversation and for trading jokes and good stories.

When LBJ became President in 1963, Americans lived much as they do today, but in 1908, when he was born, people lived more like pioneers. Television and airplanes did not exist. On the farms near Stonewall, Texas, where he was born, no one had electric lights or dishwashers or even indoor toilets or bathtubs and sinks with running water. They owned no telephones or cars. The Johnsons worked hard on their farm. Lyndon's father Sam plowed fields, slopped hogs, chopped wood, and hauled dozens of buckets of water into the house for bathing and cleaning and cooking. His mother Rebekah fed chickens, grew vegetables, sewed the family's clothes, cooked in a fireplace, and scrubbed the floor on her hands and knees. Chores on a farm never ended.

When baby Lyndon arrived, on August 27, 1908, his proud father rode his horse Fritz to the houses of family and friends nearby to announce the news. Lyndon's mother was equally thrilled; she was not used to the work of a farmer's wife, and the birth of her first son made her hard life on a farm seem worthwhile. Before her marriage she had lived in town, graduated from Baylor University, taught public speaking, and reported for the newspaper. Both her college education and her working at a paid job were highly unusual for a young woman at that time.

Two years after Lyndon's birth he had a little sister. Every two years after that another Johnson baby was born until there were five: Lyndon, Rebekah, Josepha, Sam Houston, and Lucia.

Lyndon stayed close to his mother as a small child and to his father as he got older. He said that his mother "kept me constantly amused. I remember playing games with her only the two of us could play," and another time he remembered, "She needed me to take care of her. It made me believe I could do anything in the whole world." Rebekah saw how bright her little boy was and taught him to read and to recite poetry long before he was old enough to attend school. She loved to read grown-up books to him like the poetry of John Milton and the novels of Charles Dickens, and she told him stories from the Bible and history and mythology and about her own childhood.

When he was four or five years old, Lyndon's parents had a disagreement. His hair was long and hung in ringlets, which his mother thought were beautiful. His father, though, said, "You're making a sissy of him." While his mother was at church one day, his father cut off his curls. Rebekah Johnson did not speak to her husband for a week.

About this time the Johnson family left the farm and moved, not far, into Johnson City, a town of 323 people, where young Lyndon's father went into the real estate business and his mother taught debating in the high school. When business was not good for Sam Johnson, they returned for a few years to farm life. While they lived on the farm, young Lyndon rode a mule to a school that taught about 60 children of all ages in one room.

The Johnson children did chores, but the younger brother and sisters remembered that Lyndon didn't work as much as they did; he was bossy, telling them what to do. Sometimes, if they resisted, he bribed them with cookies. His brother Sam Houston, six years younger, remembered that at other times Lyndon was protective of him and that he taught him how to play dominoes and to ride a bike.

At school Lyndon often got in trouble for playing practical jokes or acting like a clown or not doing his homework. He found it hard to sit still to do his work, but his mother was determined he should. She would ask him in the morning if his lessons were prepared. If they were not, she read them to him during breakfast and even walked to school with him, continuing to read aloud, until the studying was completed.

Not only was Lyndon's father Sam a farmer and a real estate man, he also was elected as a legislator, helping to pass laws for the State of Texas. By the time he was ten years old, Lyndon had discovered something that he did love to study— his father's world of politics. He thrilled to go with him to the Texas capitol building in Austin, where he listened for hours as the legislators discussed the state's business. Often he wandered the halls of the capitol trying to figure out what this world of government was all about. In election years he proudly traveled with his father to the towns in the Central Texas Hill Country, listening to him make speeches explaining why people should vote for him to represent them in the legislature. At night he hung around near the porch just to watch his father and his father's friends drink beer, play dominoes, talk about politics, and tell jokes and stories. That became one of Lyndon's favorite ways to spend an evening even while he was President.

After he graduated from the 11th grade (the last grade of high school at that time), 15-year-old Lyndon had no idea how he wanted to spend his adult life. His parents thought he should go to college, but he said later, "Something told me I'd go to pieces if I went to college. I'd just finished ten years of sitting inside a school; the prospect of another four years was awful." Instead, he decided to drive to California with four friends to see what living in another part of the United States was like. Because he was afraid to tell his family that he was not obeying their wishes, he sneaked out of the house one morning before they woke up and was off on his first independent adventure. His angry father, when he learned what his son had done, called sheriffs of nearly every county between Johnson City and the New Mexico border, telling them to arrest Lyndon and send him back home, but the boys were not caught. Lyndon's mother reacted more sympathetically. She called his aunt in Fredericksburg and told her that Lyndon had forgotten to take a pillow with him and would she please loan him one if he stopped at her house. The boy-on-the-run did not stop at his aunt's house.

The friends drove ten days to reach California, getting lost along the way and making a side trip to see the Grand Canyon. Because they didn't have much money, they camped out rather than stay in hotels. What little money they had they buried each time they rested, and one of them slept on top of the loose dirt in case they were robbed. At one stop they had to shoot a rattlesnake before they could lie down to sleep.

The boys arrived in California with only $8. Fortunately, Lyndon had a cousin in San Bernardino he could stay with while he looked for a job. The work he found was meager: washing dishes, waiting on tables, herding goats, running errands for a law office.

Finally, discouraged and homesick, he went back to Texas. His parents again argued and pleaded with him to go to college, but he again refused. He found a job laboring on a construction crew building a highway. Working in the hot Texas sun with his hands was hard and unsatisfying. Slowly, on his own, he began to realize that his high school education was not enough learning to get him the kind of life he wanted. Thinking he might like to become a teacher, he enrolled in Southwest Texas State Teacher's College in San Marcos, 50 miles from home.

That first year in college Lyndon was homesick, as he had been in California, and he struggled academically and financially, but he was determined to stay. He studied history and education. He disliked physical education, and he made his lowest grade in P.E. By this time he was tall and thin and had black, wavy hair. He walked fast and talked fast, and he seemed as if he were always in a hurry to get somewhere. Like his father, he was friendly and loved to talk to anyone he saw. He especially enjoyed discussing politics, and he loved telling stories to amuse his friends. All his life he was a good storyteller.

Lyndon lacked money for college, so he worked after class each day to pay for his education. His jobs as a janitor and a messenger boy did not pay enough to cover classes and food and a room to live in, however, so he left school to earn the money he needed. He got a job as a teacher of fifth, sixth, and seventh graders in the dusty little town of Cotulla, Texas, where the temperature could rise to 110 degrees and there were no shade trees to stand under. His students' families, mostly Hispanic, lived lives of poverty greater than he had ever seen before. They lacked so much that makes for a healthy, promising life, and discrimination was their daily bread. Young Lyndon Johnson responded with a fierce desire to help them make their lives better, and he carried, for the rest of his life, the memory of their struggle just to get by —until, finally, as President, he could introduce a group of laws on their behalf, which he called the War on Poverty.

Twenty-year-old Lyndon taught in Cotulla and saved his money until he had enough to return to San Marcos and finish college. Finally, with a diploma in hand, he was ready for the adult world. He thought about the kind of person he had become and what he wanted to do with his life. He never tired of working. He was happiest when talking to people and solving problems. He wanted to help those whose lives were difficult. He especially loved the workings of government, which he had learned from watching his father. He wanted to be a leader. He knew that politics was the right career for him.

1924, Lyndon is 16 years old

Twenty-year old Lyndon teaches 5th, 6th,
and 7th graders in Cotulla, Texas

Twenty-six year old Lyndon sends his photograph
to Lady Bird Taylor

## CHAPTER II

## *Lyndon Goes to Washington*

LIKE MANY YOUNG PEOPLE AT the start of their careers, Lyndon Johnson was not sure how to begin. He returned to teaching, this time in a Houston high school, but he remained interested in politics and government, so after work, at night, he volunteered to help a Texan named Richard Kleberg in his campaign to be elected to Congress. Congressmen represent their neighbors in Washington, D. C. just as Lyndon's father had represented his neighbors in Austin in the Texas Legislature. When Mr. Kleberg won the election, he offered 23-year-old Lyndon a job running his office in Washington. LBJ's career in politics, which would last a lifetime, had now begun.

He worked seven days a week at his new job, beginning at 7 o'clock in the morning and often ending as late as midnight, and he expected everyone around him to work hard also. He sent part of his salary home each month to help his parents.

The first decision he made about how to be a good politician was that it was important to know as many people as possible who worked in government. He lived in a building with many other young men who were congressional aides, and he tried to know them all. He made a plan. They all shared a large bathroom, and when he first arrived, he took four showers one night and brushed his teeth five different times the next morning. He knew that the other aides would come in to shower and brush their teeth, and if he stayed in the bathroom long enough, he would meet everyone. He looked for other ways to meet government workers who did not live in his building.

The second thing he learned about politics was the importance of knowing the people back in Texas who voted. When the time came for the next election, he traveled back and forth across the part of the state Mr. Kleberg represented, meeting hundreds of people and telling them about his boss.

Lyndon was now 26 years old. One day in Austin a friend introduced him to a young woman who had recently graduated from the University of Texas. Her name was Claudia Taylor, but everyone called her Lady Bird. She said later that being with Lyndon "was just like finding yourself in the middle of a whirlwind" because, on their first date, he told her so much about his family, his job, and his dreams for his life, and he peppered her with questions about herself. They began that first date with breakfast at the Driskill Hotel in Austin. Then they drove around Austin and into the nearby hills, talking, all day long. Before the end of the day he asked her to marry him. Shocked, she replied, "You must be joking." Nevertheless, he continued to propose over and over, and ten weeks later she married this man whom she called "the most outspoken, straightforward, determined young man I'd ever met." Without telling their families, they drove to San Antonio, and in a lavender dress Lady Bird wed Lyndon at St. Mark's Episcopal Church. Afterward, with 12 friends, they dined and danced at the St. Anthony Hotel. Their next 38 years together were, indeed, a "whirlwind."

The young woman who married Lyndon Johnson became the anchor in his life. She matched his restless charging-ahead to get things done with her own ever-patient and calm judgment and a softness he needed at the end of a hurly-burly day. Lady Bird grew up in East Texas in a more Southern and graceful world than the hard-scrabble Texas Hill Country that Lyndon had known. Her mother died when she was five years old, and the little girl, though well cared for in a big house, had to learn about loneliness at an early age. As a child she walked in the woods and the flower-strewn fields near her home in Karnack, Texas, and there she developed a deep love for nature. She did well in school and went on to college, graduating at a time when four times more young men attended college than young women.

Lyndon became restless at his job running a congressional office. He dreamed of being a congressman himself. He noticed that many congressmen were lawyers, so he went to law school at night for a short time. He quit because he thought the school did not teach him any practical ways to solve problems that he did not already know. Then he found a job he wanted back in Texas. He applied to President Franklin Roosevelt for appointment as Director of the National Youth Administration in Austin. At first President Roosevelt feared that, at 26, Lyndon was too young for the job, but he decided to give him a chance. The NYA helped young people finish school if they did not have money and to find jobs when jobs were scarce. Lyndon wanted every young person to be able to learn and to work and to have the best life possible. He started the new youth program with his usual gusto, working his staff seven days a week, late into the night. He loved his job because he was helping people, but he worked so hard and got so little sleep that he often was sick with colds or the flu and several times with pneumonia. He did such a good job that Eleanor Roosevelt, the President's wife, made several trips to Texas to observe how he was running the NYA so that she could pass on his ideas to other directors around the country. She and the President decided that, even though he was young himself, Lyndon Johnson knew how to help young people better than anyone else in the United States.

Finally, his chance came to run for office. The Congressman from his district in Texas died. Lyndon had his heart set on running, but he would have to quit his job, and he had no money. Lady Bird believed in her husband; she made the first contribution to his campaign with $10,000 inherited from her family. Eight other people announced their candidacy for the same race, but Lyndon believed he could beat them all if he met enough voters. He drove throughout his district every day talking and shaking hands. When he saw a farmer in the field, he climbed the fence and talked to him. When he drove by a service station, he bought a gallon of gasoline and met everyone at the station. He walked down the main street of small towns, stopping people to tell them who he was. After six weeks he was exhausted and sick with appendicitis. He spent the last few days of the campaign in the hospital having his appendix removed. While he was recovering he learned that he had been elected to Congress. His hard work had paid off. Lyndon and Lady Bird were moving back to Washington. This time, rather than working for a congressman from Texas, he would *be* a congressman from Texas.

Lady Bird and Lyndon honeymoon in Mexico

1941, Congressman Johnson becomes a Naval officer
in World War II

# CHAPTER III

## *Congressman Johnson*

LYNDON JOHNSON HAD long recognized that he could learn from experienced men who were older than he was. In Congress he gained two mentors who helped him understand government and politics in all their complexity. One was President Franklin D. Roosevelt, who saw into the future when he said about LBJ, "This boy could well be the first southern President." The other mentor was a fellow Texan named Sam Rayburn, who was the leader of the U.S. House of Representatives. His title was Speaker of the House. The two men worked together all week at the Capitol, and almost every Sunday Mr. Rayburn ate dinner with the Johnsons. They remained close friends throughout their lives.

Congressman Johnson continued his habit of working until he was exhausted and sick and of pushing his staff equally hard. He insisted that they answer every letter from a voter back home the day it came into the office. Paying attention to the problems of the people who voted for you was what got you re-elected, he told them. He also continued trying to know well all the Congressmen and government workers he dealt with. He raised money for many Democratic Congressmen who were facing elections they might not win without some help. He employed a young Texan, John

Connally, as his aide. John Connally later became governor of Texas and ran for President himself.

One of Lyndon's proudest accomplishments as a congressman was that he helped get dams built across the rivers in Central Texas so that his neighbors in the country would have electricity and their land would not flood. Their lives would be easier. One Texan remembers coming home after dark to see light inside her house for the first time. Such a sight, unlike anything she had ever seen before, made her fear that her house was on fire.

Congressman Johnson became restless again. He hoped to be a U.S. senator and to represent his entire state instead of a small section as he was doing now. He would rather be one of 96 senators than one of 435 representatives, but he lost the senate race to the colorful governor of Texas, W. Lee "Pappy" O'Daniel, who had been a hillbilly singer and whose motto was, "Pass the biscuits, Pappy," because he had sold flour before he was governor. Lyndon tried mightily; he had support from President Roosevelt, and he even hired a band himself to campaign with him. After the election, Lyndon Johnson was declared the winner until some uncounted votes came in that made O'Daniel the new senator by a little over 1,000 votes. No doubt, the election had not been honest, but in those days election rules were not enforced strictly. Lyndon tried to hide his heartbreak. Shortly after the election Lady Bird said, "His head was high, and he was stepping along real spryly. I know how much nerve and effort were now required for him to keep up that courageous appearance." He later described the days after the lost election as the most miserable in his life.

America by now had entered World War II, fighting the Germans in Europe and the Japanese across the Pacific Ocean. Congressman Johnson joined the Navy and went to the Pacific while Mrs. Johnson ran his congressional office in Washington.

After her husband returned, Lady Bird Johnson, who had spent part of her inheritance to pay for LBJ's congressional campaign, now chose to invest more of it in a radio station in Austin called KTBC. For many years she worked to make KTBC a profitable radio station, and, later, a successful television and radio business. People who worked with her appreciated her close attention to every little detail of how the station operated and how it spent its money. She often traveled between Washington, D.C. and Austin juggling her jobs as a business person and a congressional wife.

In the next few years the Johnsons' lives changed in important ways. Their first daughter, Lynda Bird, was born. President Roosevelt died, and Harry S. Truman became President. The war ended. Then a second daughter, Lucy Baines, arrived. When LBJ was 40 years old, he ran for the Senate a second time even though he was afraid he would be beaten. He had been badly hurt when he lost before, but he decided that he wanted to be a senator and so must try again.

As a congressman he had represented people only in Central Texas, but as a senator he would have to win the votes of a majority of all Texans. Once again he tried to meet as many voters as possible, but this time the job was more difficult because he would be covering the entire state. He decided he could meet the challenge by traveling in a helicopter, an aircraft rarely seen in those days. He flew to 118 towns in 17 days, and the crowds flocked to this unusual sight. As his craft hovered in the air, he would shout over a loudspeaker, "Hello down there. This is Lyndon Johnson, your candidate for the U. S. Senate." Then, after he landed and opened the helicopter's door, he would toss his Stetson hat into the crowd. People usually whooped and hollered in response as if they were at a rodeo or a football game. While he shook their hands, his aides would have to hunt for the hat and sometimes pay a dollar to the person who had caught it in order to get it back.

When the race was over, Lyndon Johnson had defeated Governor Coke Stevenson by only 87 votes. Both sides claimed the other had played unfairly in order to win. People are still arguing the question.

1948, A helicopter is a new way of campaigning for office

Future Supreme Court Justice Abe Fortas
receives the "Johnson Treatment"

# CHAPTER IV

## *Senator Johnson*

IN THE SENATE, Lyndon Johnson's big, exuberant personality and his high intelligence and his devotion to work came together to produce what many have called the most effective leader of the Senate in American history. To understand how he achieved such success, let us first see how he became the Senate's leader.

He did the four things he had done in every new job. First, he found a mentor, Senator Richard Russell from Georgia, who instructed him on the workings of the Senate and who became his lifelong friend. Lyndon Johnson was looking for someone to teach him and someone to help him solve problems by talking them over together. He and Senator Russell spent their weekdays at work and their weekends at the Johnsons' home together. Second, the new Senator Johnson studied avidly how to do his job. He thought he must know everything about the problems that he would vote on for the country and he must understand the rules of the Senate. He was thirsty for information and could never get enough. Third, he set out to know well the people he worked with, from how they felt about bills before the Congress to the names of their children. Finally, he worked harder than anyone else. Sometimes he would work around the clock, napping a few hours in his office and asking Lady Bird to bring him fresh clothes from home in the morning.

His devotion catapulted him to the head of the Senate within a few years. The party that contains more than half the members of the Senate is called the majority party. Its powerful leader is named Majority Leader. The party with fewer members is known as the minority party, and its leader is called the Minority Leader. When Lyndon Johnson first went to the Senate, the Democrats were the minority party. Within three years they had named him their Minority Leader. Another three years passed, and they became the majority party. They chose LBJ as Majority Leader.

He thought it was important in this job for Democrats and Republicans to work well with each other and for the Senate to work well with President Dwight Eisenhower, who was a Republican. LBJ promoted bipartisanship, which means Republicans and Democrats trying to find ways to agree so that they could pass laws satisfactory to both. Regularly the two Democrats—Majority Leader Lyndon Johnson and Speaker of the House Sam Rayburn— met secretly with President Eisenhower at the White House and talked about ways the two political parties could help the country together. When asked about this unusual cooperation between leaders of opposing parties, Senator Johnson said of President Eisenhower, "If you're in an airplane, and you're flying somewhere, you don't run up to the cockpit and attack the pilot. Mr. Eisenhower is the only president we've got." When Senator Johnson became President, he met in the same way with Republican leader Senator Everett Dirksen. Each of these four patriots from different political parties wanted his team to win elections against the other, but they all wanted the country to be the final winner by having good laws both sides could support.

He tried to make other senators' jobs easier for them. Whether they were Democrats or Republicans, he saw to it that each got to work on a committee studying problems that really interested that person. He never asked a senator to vote in a way to make the people from his home state angry. He tried to make senators his friend by doing nice things for them: helping one to find an office employee, asking another to represent the Senate at a conference in Europe, sending congratulations on birthdays and wedding anniversaries.

He also used what became known as "the Johnson treatment" to convince people to vote with him. When he wanted something from another person, he would tower over him with their noses almost touching and overwhelm him with pleas and arguments and statistics and his booming, hypnotizing personality until that person simply wilted in the face of so much energy directed at him from such close range. One newspaper man said it was "as if a St. Bernard had licked your face for an hour, had pawed you all over." That was "the Johnson treatment." It was very dramatic, and it was effective.

It was during the senate years that Lyndon and Lady Bird bought from his aunt and uncle their ranch, where Lyndon remembered spending happy Christmases and summer holidays as a child in Texas. This land was hilly and rocky; it was peppered with cattle and deer and live oak and pecan trees and rivers and creeks that flooded one year and struggled to stay moist the next, and it fed him as surely as food. As he rose in power and responsibility within the government, he found it necessary to his well-being to return there often, where he said the land and the people refreshed and inspired him as nothing else could. Lady Bird simply said, "It is our heart's home."

People were suggesting that Lyndon Johnson should be President of the United States until a serious problem stopped him in his tracks. When he was 47 years old, he suffered a heart attack. After he left the hospital, many months passed before he could work again.

When he did return to the Senate, the important question of segregation faced the country. African-Americans had begun objecting strenuously to segregation. In many states there were laws which said they could not sit side by side with whites on buses and trains and that they must use separate restrooms and water fountains and go to different schools from whites. This was called the Civil Rights issue. LBJ, all his life, had hated that his part of the country believed in segregation. He cared passionately that everyone should have equal opportunity for good jobs and to any seat on the bus and to the same schools. The beginnings of discussion about this most serious problem in America and the first small steps toward passing laws to make blacks and whites full partners began at this time. After Johnson became President, more laws would help make civil rights in America a reality.

Then the Soviet Union shocked Americans by launching a man into space in a satellite called Sputnik. Americans already feared the power of the Soviet Union, a country then unfriendly to the United States. Lyndon Johnson was at his Texas ranch when he heard the news. He walked outside and stared at the sky in amazement, both at the wonder of man conquering space and at the fact that another nation, especially a feared one, would be the one to do so first. He became the leader in convincing Americans that we, too, could soar in space and that we must. He saw to it that a law passed creating NASA, the National Aeronautics and Space Administration, to help America surpass the Soviet Union at space exploration.

Since his graduation from college, Lyndon Johnson had been a school teacher, an aide to a congressman, a congressman himself, and a senator. Next he would become Vice-President of the United States.

Senator and Mrs. Johnson buy a ranch near Stonewall, Texas,
where they eventually retire

1961, Vice President Johnson shakes hands with a camel driver
in Pakistan whom he invites to visit the United States

# CHAPTER V

## *Vice President Johnson*

IN 1960 THE Democrats chose John Fitzgerald Kennedy as their candidate for President, and he asked Lyndon Johnson to be his running mate as Vice-President. The two men were elected, but soon Lyndon Johnson realized that he disliked being Vice-President. He no longer was in a position to make decisions for his country. He could only stand by and watch others make those important choices. He had thrived on being a leader, and now he was reduced to being an assistant to someone else's leadership.

Representing the President, he spent much of his time flying to other countries telling people about democracy in America. As Vice-President, he traveled to 33 countries, where he mostly shook hands and made speeches when what he longed to do was to solve problems. A meeting with an unexpected outcome occurred while the Vice-President was in Pakistan. Vice-President Johnson saw a man standing beside his camel along the side of a road. He shook the surprised man's hand and said casually, "Come to see us." To the Vice-President's astonishment, the camel-driver took him seriously and accepted. Rather than back down on an invitation he had meant to be friendly but not real, the Vice-President brought the camel-driver, who spoke no English, back to the United States and entertained him in Texas and Washington, D. C. and New York while the world watched on television, delighted with this unusual bit of foreign diplomacy.

Back home Vice-President Johnson concentrated on the space program. He met with scientists and with military and political and business leaders on the problems of space travel. Then he reported to the President that, although it would be very expensive, America should send a man to the moon, and shortly after he left the presidency, America did land astronauts on the moon. It was a proud day for the United States.

He also continued while he was Vice-President to devote his time to civil rights. He and President Kennedy objected to black Americans not being given their fair chance in a democracy. Meanwhile, many whites, especially in the South where the majority of blacks lived, were so used to the old ways of doing things that they saw no need to change. Vice-President Johnson felt angry and frustrated that many people would not listen to him when he tried to convince them that this was wrong.

Finally, the Vice-President's job was made difficult by the fact that he and President Kennedy's brother, Robert Kennedy, did not like each other. Robert Kennedy was Attorney General, the lawyer for the country. The two men had to work together often, and neither was happy about it.

On November 22, 1963, a terrible thing happened. President Kennedy and Vice-President Johnson and their wives went to Texas so that the President could raise money for his upcoming re-election campaign. In Dallas, at about noon, they were driving slowly through the city streets in open-topped cars, waving to welcoming crowds. The day was sunny; people from Dallas were excited to have a president in their city. Suddenly, a gun fired. From the sixth floor of a building along the parade route, a man named Lee Harvey Oswald had shot President Kennedy. In the car in which Lyndon and Lady Bird Johnson were riding, a brave Secret Service agent named Rufus Youngblood was sitting in the front seat while the Johnsons were in the back. He heard the shots. "Get down, get down," he yelled to the Vice-President as he leaped over the front seat and threw his own body on top of Vice-President Johnson to protect him from harm. The car sped behind President Kennedy's car to the hospital, where the Johnsons soon learned that President Kennedy had died. That same afternoon they, along with Mrs. Kennedy and a casket carrying President Kennedy's body, boarded the presidential airplane, Air Force One. Inside the airplane Lyndon Johnson, only one hour and 30 minutes after the President's death, was sworn in as the 36th President of the United States. By evening President Johnson was back in his Washington office, working into the night at his new job to be sure the world knew that the United States still had a leader to guide it. Before he went to bed that night he wrote a note to each of President Kennedy's two young children, Caroline and John, to tell them how sad their father's death had made him.

A few days later the sorrowing new President went to the Capitol and, in a speech before Congress, said, "All I have I would have given gladly not to be standing here today."

At first the Johnsons remained in their own house because they kindly told Jacqueline Kennedy to take as long as she needed to move from the White House to a new home, and even after they moved in, they welcomed young Caroline Kennedy and her 20 classmates to continue to have kindergarten in the family quarters until the end of the semester

President and Mrs. Johnson knew it was important to draw their family close together to help one another adjust to and enjoy this unique and puzzling life that had been thrust upon them. Nineteen-year-old Lynda moved out of her dormitory at The University of Texas in Austin and into the White House and transferred to nearby Georgetown University. Luci, who had changed the spelling of her name from "Lucy" to "Luci," was 16 and still in high school. She and Lynda filled the family living quarters on the second and third floors of the White House with cookie baking and spend-the-night friends and birthday parties and, finally, romance, as each became a young adult and married. Then their two husbands left for active military service in Vietnam, and the sisters remained in the White House, now each with a small child. During the years of his presidency, these children and grandchildren gave Lyndon Johnson the laughter and love and encouragement he needed in the midst of his grueling days trying to solve overwhelming national and international problems. When tired and discouraged, the President found pleasure and relief in letting his grandson play with the telephone in his office or in dashing from the Oval Office to the next-door living quarters for a quick lunch with his wife and daughters.

1963, The family is photographed a few days after Lyndon Johnson becomes President

1968, The President often has one of his dogs with him,
even in the Oval Office

# CHAPTER VI

## *President Johnson:  Passing Laws*

LYNDON JOHNSON IMAGINED an America that he called The Great Society.  In The Great Society poor people would be helped to find jobs, old people would receive health care even if they could not pay for it, and any child who had the ability could go to college.  Theaters and orchestras and operas would be enjoyed, not just in a few big cities, but across the country and on television.  The air and water around us would be kept clean and pure, and new national parks would be established.  Most importantly, in The Great Society, hotels and restaurants and playgrounds and houses and apartments would no longer be for "whites only," as signs outside their doors sometimes read, and blacks would vote as freely as whites.  All Americans would share the good things in their country in ways they never had before.

When he became President, Lyndon Johnson went to work energetically to make these dreams come true. He appointed 14 different committees to come up with ideas of how to make the country even better, and then he presented many of their suggestions to Congress. Some feared these new projects would be too expensive, and some believed they would encourage the government to interfere too much in people's lives.  His plans, however, were agreed to by a majority in Congress, and they passed into law and have made the lives of millions of Americans safer, longer, and more productive.

As to civil rights, the proposed new laws said no one could be refused a job or kept out of a public place because of the color of his skin; no state could keep poor people from voting by charging them a tax as the price of voting; and no one could be denied a place to live because of his race. In working to make civil rights a reality, President Johnson formed an important partnership with Dr. Martin Luther King, Jr., a black minister from the South, who believed that America would change its segregationist laws if blacks and sympathetic whites simply showed up in huge numbers at public places to demonstrate how strongly they felt and how many of them there were. Most famously, he led a 54-mile march of protesters from Selma, Alabama to Montgomery, Alabama. Because some people, angry at the protests, became violent, President Johnson sent U.S. soldiers to Alabama to line the parade route and see that these peaceful protesters were not harmed. Dr. King said in a famous speech, "I have a dream that one day on the red hills of Georgia the sons of former slaves and the sons of former slave owners will be able to sit down together at the table of brotherhood."

The two men, Johnson and King, met in the White House to discuss their plans, and while Dr. King was inspiring his people to insist on their rights and to be unafraid of people who threatened them, President Johnson was forcing the passage of civil rights laws by convincing enough congressmen to vote for them at a time when many did not want to and by never giving up until the job was done.

In education, money from Washington was given to schools throughout the country for the first time. The money helped young people of all ages whose families were poor. A program called Head Start offered nursery school and kindergarten classes. Money for older children was used to purchase classroom materials and to help pay for special education and to teach students in their native language if they could not speak English. College-age young people who needed financial help were offered scholarships and loans.

Because he had never forgotten the poor people he had known when he had taught school in Cotulla as a young man, President Johnson began a program called The War on Poverty. It started the Job Corps, which helped train young people so they could get jobs.

His concern for the health problems of older Americans made him begin Medicare, which helped people pay for medical services in the last years of their lives.

He started the National Endowment for the Arts and the National Endowment for the Humanities and the Public Broadcasting System, all of which said that because the arts and learning were important in people's lives, they should be supported by the government.

Also, he cared about the environment. During his presidency 35 new national parks were established and thousands of miles of hiking trails. Mrs. Johnson contributed, also, in ways that expressed her own love of nature and her concern for protecting it. She was behind a bill which limited billboards and hid junk yards along the sides of the highways. She tried to make Washington a model city the rest of the country could copy by beautifying Pennsylvania Avenue, which ran from the White House to the Capitol; by creating parks throughout the city; by planting gardens full of daffodils and pink dogwood trees like she had known in East Texas; and by cleaning up poor neighborhoods. She also took 40 strenuous trips into wilderness areas to make the public aware of the treasure they were for the country.

In the midst of all this bill passing, President Johnson had to run for re-election. Senator Hubert Humphrey of Minnesota was his running mate as Vice-President. Lyndon Johnson won the majority vote in 44 of the 50 states, and more people voted for him than had ever voted for a president before, but in a few years, he would be a very unpopular President because of the war in Vietnam.

1966, The President and Martin Luther King, Jr.
ponder the issue of Civil Rights

1968, When the President leaves the Oval Office,
he continues working in the family quarters

1968, President Johnson listens to a tape sent by his son-in-law, Captain Charles Robb, who was serving in Vietnam

## CHAPTER VII

# *President Johnson: Fighting a War*

ONE TERRIBLE PROBLEM overwhelmed Lyndon Johnson's presidency: communism in a country called Vietnam, 10,00 miles away.

Communism intends for everyone to own everything together so that no one person has more possessions than another. Its government divides up what the people have, and it tells people what they must do without and where they must live and work. In China, the Communist Government even controls how many children they may have. That government is not elected, so it cannot be overturned if the people disagree with its decisions. Citizens are not allowed to complain.

When Lyndon Johnson was President, communism was on the move throughout the world. The Communists openly scorned American democracy, and they tried to convince other countries to become communist. America treasured its freedom for people to choose how they wanted to live, and they loved its elections in which they picked their own government instead of having one forced on them. They feared the Communist victories in other parts of the world.

Two huge countries—the Soviet Union and China—already had turned to communism. A small country, Vietnam, which was right next to China, was struggling to decide which form of government it would choose. The Communist North Vietnam was fighting the Democratic South Vietnam for control of its government. Many people in America believed that if all of Vietnam became communist, it would convince other countries to do the same. The fall of each country to communism would make another country fall, in turn, like lined-up dominoes, until there was no place left for democracy. This view is known as The Domino Theory.

At first, America sent military men to Vietnam to teach the Democratic South Vietnamese how to fight the Communist North Vietnamese. The Americans themselves did not fight. They only advised. Then, one Sunday morning, three North Vietnamese torpedo boats attacked an American ship called The Maddox, which was lying 16 miles off the shore of Vietnam. The Maddox fought back, sinking one of the torpedo boats. Later North Vietnam attacked some American military advisors, killing 8 of them, and again America made an attack of their own in response. Soon the Americans and the South Vietnamese were fighting side by side against the North Vietnamese. Most Americans thought the President had made the right decision to fight. As time went by, however, many Americans began to believe the war could not be won and that no American soldier should die over a small country on the other side of the world. No one knew what the future would hold if America continued to fight in Vietnam or if it left Vietnam.

Those who thought the war had to be fought were called Hawks, and those who believed the war was wrong were called Doves. An argument raged between the two. Many families were torn between parents and children who disagreed. Sometimes young men who were told they must be drafted into the army ran away to another country rather than fight. Those who protested the war held rallies, and thousands of people showed up. Those who supported the war called the protesters unpatriotic, and fights sometimes broke out. Every day people marched outside the White House shouting against the war, and whenever the President went out in public, they called out to him. One particularly harsh slogan chanted as he passed by was, "Hey, hey, LBJ, how many boys did you kill today?" At night, inside the White House, that cry could still be heard by all the family; it was especially painful to Lynda and Luci, whose husbands were in Vietnam on active duty. America was not at peace with itself.

President Johnson was torn between thinking the war against communism must be won and not being sure it was possible to win. The safety of the world was so important, yet the deaths of American military men so heart-breaking, and his fear for his two sons-in-law at the war front so distressing, that one night he sat down with his friend, Senator Richard Russell, and cried.

It came time for the President once again to run for election. More and more Americans had turned against the war. Lyndon Johnson, who understood politics so well, realized that he had lost the backing of a large portion of the country. He could see that the war was at a stalemate: no matter how many troops the Americans sent into Vietnam, the communists continued to send more, and there seemed no end in sight. He also feared that his health would not allow him to serve out another term in office, and he did not want the country to face a crisis if his health failed. He counted the cost of the war in lives lost and money and attention diverted from solving America's problems at home. He decided, after struggling with the decision for months, that nothing was more important—not even being elected President of the United States—than to spend all his waking hours searching for an honorable end to the war. He must not, at the same time, conduct a backbreaking campaign for office that would drain his energies and further divide the American people.

And so, on March 31, 1968, Lyndon Johnson went on national television and said to a shocked audience, "With America's sons in the fields far away, with America's future under challenge right here at home, with our hopes and the world's hopes for peace in the balance every day, I do not believe that I should devote an hour or a day of my time to any personal partisan causes or to any duties other than the awesome duties of this office—the Presidency of your country. Accordingly, I shall not seek, and I will not accept, the nomination of my party for another term as your President."

President Johnson still had ten more months to serve, and as the year proceeded, strife within the country was greater than ever. Before the year was over, both 39-year-old Martin Luther King, Jr. and 42-year-old Robert Kennedy were assassinated, and student and civil rights protests escalated into repeated violence. In Washington the President had to put soldiers on the street to protect citizens. He called this "the nightmare year." One thrilling event, however, in December of 1968, unrelated to war abroad and unrest within the country, broke the spell of gloom. Just before Christmas Apollo 8 took off from the Kennedy Space Center, and, while half a billion people watched on television, the three American astronauts orbited the moon just 60 miles from its surface. One of the photographs they brought back—of the earth as seen from space—served to remind people of the beauty of this world and our need to care for it. President Johnson had played a crucial role in promoting the space program since its beginning, and in the next year he would have the deep satisfaction of seeing Apollo 11 actually land on the moon and Americans walk its surface.

On January 20, 1969, Republican Richard Nixon entered the White House as the 37th President, and Lady Bird and Lyndon went home to their ranch in Texas and to retirement.

The hard days are interspersed with happy family ones
like Luci's graduation from high school in 1965 and Lynda's
marriage to Charles Robb in 1967

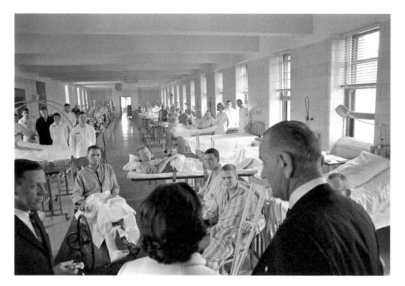

President and Mrs. Johnson go to the hospital to visit
servicemen wounded in Vietnam

"Earthrise," a photograph taken of the earth from Apollo 8, as it orbited the mooon

President and Mrs. Johnson retire to their
ranch near Stonewall, Texas

# CHAPTER VIII

# The End of A Life of Service

ON RICHARD NIXON'S inauguration day, Lyndon and Lady Bird Johnson watched him be sworn in on the Capitol grounds as the new President of the United States. At a farewell lunch the Johnsons sadly said good-bye to friends they had made through the many years they had lived in Washington. Then they helicoptered to Andrews Air Force Base where the presidential plane waited to fly them one last time to Texas. When they landed at Bergstrom Air Force Base in Austin, 5,000 Texans welcomed them with banners and bouquets of flowers. The University of Texas Longhorn Band played "The Eyes of Texas." Finally, they took one last flight in a smaller plane to the LBJ ranch, arriving just at dark. Thirty-two years of public service in Washington lay behind them, and they had come home to their beloved Hill Country to stay.

For the next four years the former President embraced life as energetically and passionately as ever. On the campus of the University of Texas at Austin, he oversaw the construction of both a presidential library that would contain all the papers of his presidency and a school to prepare students for careers in public service. (Today over 200,000 people visit the LBJ Library and Museum each year and more than 300 students study at the LBJ School of Public

Affairs). He wrote a book about his presidency. He saw to it that a nursing home named after his mother was built in Austin as an example of how to care for old people properly. He watched over his ranch, seeing that the cattle were tended and the fences were mended. He often invited friends to visit. He liked to drive them about the ranch before dinner, pointing out the white-tailed deer. Later in the evening he and his guests often sat on lawn chairs in the front yard under a huge live oak tree trading stories about politics and growing up in the Hill Country. Sometimes he played dominoes just as his father and his friends had done over 50 years before. He let his hair, now white where it had once been black, grow to his shoulders. The immensity of the problems he had faced as President showed on his face; he looked much older than he was. He began to have heart trouble again.

Four years after he returned to Texas—on January 22, 1973—Lyndon Johnson's heart stopped beating. Following a funeral in Washington, D. C., the 64-year old President's body was returned to the Texas Hill Country he loved, and on a bitterly cold and rainy winter day he was buried in the family cemetery within sight of the house in which he had been born, alongside his parents and his brother and sisters. Thirty-four years later Lady Bird was laid to rest beside him.

Just a month before his death, President Johnson had thrilled to one last proud occasion when hundreds of men and women interested in the civil rights movement came to his presidential library, the LBJ Library, in Austin to discuss how blacks and whites could continue to work toward equal opportunities for everyone. He told them, "The progress has been much too small; we haven't done nearly enough." The can-do President, even in illness, wanted to work harder and do more until all Americans, in his words, "stand on level and equal ground." That was Lyndon Johnson's dream.

His other dream—for every child to get "as much education as he has the ability to take"—was honored thirty-four years after his death when, in 2007, Congress voted to rename the Education Building in Washington D. C. the Lyndon Baines Johnson Education Building. This was a fitting tribute to the President who passed 66 education laws and who was proud that he had once been a teacher himself.

With his can-do spirit, Lyndon Johnson had changed America. Although his hope for a world safe from communism had brought pain to the nation and to him, he did get to see his country become more welcoming to people of all races and more concerned with young people's education. Those are the two accomplishments for which he would have liked to be remembered.

1973, after the President's death, mourners pass the American and Texas flags at half mast as they enter the LBJ Library in Austin to pay their respects

# Bibliography

These books, primarily intended for adult readers, offer valuable help in understanding Lyndon Johnson.

Dallek, Robert, *Lyndon B. Johnson: Portrait of a President,* Oxford University Press, 2004

Divine, Robert, edited by, *Exploring the Johnson Years,* University of Texas Press, Austin, 1981

Goodwin, Doris Kearns, *Lyndon Johnson and the American Dream,* St. Martin's Griffin, New York, 1976

Johnson, Rebekah Baines, *A Family Album,* McGraw-Hill Book Company 1965

Johnson, Sam Houston, *My Brother Lyndon,* Cowles Book Company, Inc., New York, 1969

Middleton, Harry: *LBJ: The White House Years,* Harry N. Abrams, Inc., New York, 1990

Miller, Merle, *Lyndon: An Oral Biography,* G. P. Putnam's Sons, New York, 1980

Senate Document 110-8, *First Lady Bird Johnson 1912-2007: Memorial Tributes in the One Hundred Tenth Congress of the United States,* U. S. Government Printing Office, Washington, 2008

Sinise, Jerry, *Lyndon Baines Johnson Remembered,* Eakin Press, Austin, Texas, 1985

Unger, Irwin and Unger, Debi, *LBJ: A Life,* John Wiley and Sons, Inc., 1999

Updegrove, Mark K., *Indomitable Will: LBJ in the Presidency,* Crown Publishers, New York, 2012

Woods, Randall, *LBJ: Architect of Ambition,* Free Press, New York, 2006

CPSIA information can be obtained at www.ICGtesting.com
Printed in the USA
LVIW01n1549041015
456767LV00001B/1